PRAISE FOR *GATH*

"In a world on fire, what is poetry's role? Todd Osborne's powerful debut answers this question through perfectly placed observations of ordinary moments that become extraordinary through his command of language, image, and humor. Osborne brings to the page a generous, enthusiastic, and unbridled love of the world. In *Gatherer*, 'everything feels like Mercy,' and this collection serves as a guide for finding moments of clarity, wholeness, and beauty in a time of fragmentation and loss."

—Adam Clay, author of *To Make Room for the Sea* and *Circle Back*

"Todd Osborne's gem-like debut collection exhilarates, its poems generous enough to encompass both small pleasures—the open-car-window 'zephyr' that 'wilds' the face, the fun of gathering food for an impromptu wedding-day feast—and large regrets, for the world's engrained malaise; and, more intimately, for a grandfather's long death by denaturing illness. Osborne has taken to heart Conrad's dictum: 'In the destructive element immerse.' This book is no treatise. It is both wedding song and elegy—a book of peace overriding conflict, a book of love that summons what's lost and makes of it a new and lasting beauty."

—Angela Ball, author of *Talking Pillow* and
Night Clerk at the Hotel of Both Worlds

"'Each day we survive / feels like a miracle.' Todd Osborne's lovely debut collection, *Gatherer*, wrangles so honestly and intimately with the immediacies of living and teaching and loving in the South amidst hurricanes and tornadoes, empty pandemic classrooms, and grotesque tours of antebellum mansions that avoid slavery and revel in soldiers' limbs, that you'll want to keep listening, especially to the painful silences: 'my mouth is an arm—.' Collectively, these finely wrought lyrics embody the simultaneity of disaster and love through formal flexibility: the repetition of Markov sonnets tackle living political histories, while an epithalamium turns ars poetica—'poets only write about one thing: love and how it moves within them.' Amidst this all, in the dualities, a marked vastness: of a step-ladder replacing a deck: 'If one wanted, a step into / sky; if one wanted, anything at all.'"

—Rebecca Morgan Frank, author of *Oh You Robot Saints!* and
Sometimes We're All Living in a Foreign Country

Gatherer

Gatherer

TODD OSBORNE

Poems

Fort Smith, Arkansas

GATHERER

Cover images:
Bukkende naakte man (1924) by Reijer Stolk;
Harebell (Campanula rotundifolia) (1916) and
Blue-eyed-grass (Sisyrinchium angustifolium) (1920) by Mary Vaux Walcott

Edited by Casie Dodd
Design & typography by Belle Point Press

Belle Point Press, LLC
Fort Smith, Arkansas
bellepointpress.com
editor@bellepointpress.com

Find Belle Point Press
on Facebook, Substack,
and Instagram (@bellepointpress)

Printed in the United States of America

28 27 26 25 24   1 2 3 4 5

Library of Congress Control Number: 2024930240

ISBN: 978-1-960215-16-1

GAT/BPP26

For my family, for everything
and for Mary, forever

CONTENTS

ARS POETICA

It is hard to craft a metaphor
when the world is burning.

It is difficult to construct an image
when a place you love is on fire.

When flames lick up the side of
your beloved childhood home, how

can you write about hope?

In the ashes, can you write a stanza?

When the ash is blowing all around
you, in your eyes, your lungs, your hair,
could you push through to an other side?

Say, hypothetically, you can't leave
your house for a year or more, would you
be able to look for glimmers of light

in all that darkness?

The lightbulbs in the kitchen go out
first, and the sun is blotted out—*poor air
quality*, the news says—after another

month, no light in any room, and you have
a scented candle you're not sure you can
smell anymore—*and what does that* mean?

—and you are cobbling together two lines
on a sticky note with a pencil—no eraser—so

whatever you say has to be final.

DRONE

I drove all day the day
            before, arrived in time for
the rehearsal dinner,

            early in fact, early
enough to stop
            at a coffeeshop

that even a decade before
            would not have existed—
revitalization at its finest

            —and then to the farmland
where, of course, Graham was
            to be married; it made sense,

then and now, for him to be married
            on a farm, and as I waded
through something

            that, if it wasn't actually
a cornfield, certainly feels
            like one in hindsight,

the photographer pulled a drone
            along with him and then let it
fly up and up, even let

Graham handle it a little, and
if I did not, exactly, think
of Syria, or bombs, those thoughts

were not distant
from my mind, and what I wanted
to say to Graham

after seven hours of driving
from a place where love felt far away
was perhaps love celebrated

in a field, under a tree, can last,
but maybe it shouldn't
in a world where drones can

photograph someone in one place and
photograph someone in another place and
the contexts can be

utterly opposite, and one makes
children smile and clap
their hands and the other makes

children afraid of a cloudless day,
a day like when Graham made
a vow, I witnessed it and

thought things would get better.

A HISTORY OF DECKS

Deck is gone Mom texts to me and Mo,

and shortly after a photo of the ground outside

the back door, empty of anything but a few

wooden posts, time passing. It is strange

to remember the last time this happened,

maybe 20 years ago, maybe 15, either way

enough to make the new deck warranted,

enough to make me nostalgic. My mother

cleaning out my old bedroom, and Mo's

too, and a step-ladder leading up to the back door,

and nothing more. If one wanted, a step into

sky; if one wanted, anything at all.

SNOW

Murder someone in Sevastopol in December
        and by March there will be a present left

for someone else to find. I read this in a novel;
        it is a striking image, like a lit match too close

to your face and moving closer. I want to pinch
        the flicker out, leave a slight contrail of smoke

like a corpse flowering in spring. Even this image
        is familiar. Who doesn't want to be found like this?

Face still red and, at first, one could believe
        your blood still pumps within, not without.

Saint John wrote verses about moments like that:
        the tearing away of old thoughts, the way light

finds itself breaking in to hidden places: city streets,
        subways, skulls. When given enough time, anything

will become familiar. Thousands of people walk past
        a snowbank every day, for now, and do not think

they are walking past a grave. When the snow is gone,
        so are the secrets of winter, the layers we bundle

ourselves into. We strip down to T-shirts and bloody teeth.
  We curl our biceps around a stranger's neck and leave

what's left at the bottom of a lake. It's summer's problem
  to resolve or forget. The new tradition: trawling becomes

the national pastime. I walk a street salted more
  out of hope than need. I whistle. It is a sweet sound,

I think. Like wind is an instrument. Like I can be
  unmade by the things I make. Undone by what I do.

RE:

Sometimes I believe in something like karma,
or not that, exactly, but the idea that if bad
happens to me, I probably deserve it, like the skinned
knee I received after a jog—in my apartment
complex, looking at my phone, I missed a step
I'd walked down a hundred times. Or the emails
from a group of Boise soccer parents who want
me to show up at every game—*It's very important.*
I don't want to tell them they've got the wrong guy,
I'm just an impostor with a new Comcast account.
For all the emails or text messages unreplied,
the conversations left unstarted, this is my penance:
find me sitting in bleachers 2000 miles from my home,
sweating in bright blue, praying that this is enough.

AFTER SUNLIGHT

a golden shovel after Charles Wright's "The Monastery at Vršac"

everything feels like Mercy,
the grackles hopping like nuns upon

a broken path,
                        their eyes pinned on us
as we kneel into the ground we

love, fold our hands and wonder who

will save this land next. What have
we taught each other, what learned?

The sky runs forward, to
find itself broken like the broken path, to preach
at those of us
                        with listening ears, but
not listening hearts. There is not

a reason within us, nothing to
say, no action left but to pray.

A HISTORY OF TREES

In elementary school, I had to conduct
        a Leaf Project. I visited Grandma,

        who helped me identify the leaves
in her backyard. She told me about them

and also about what happened in those
        trees at night: men gathered and burned

        God, wore white masks. *They're bad men.*
This was Tennessee in the '90s.

It is easy to believe the history books
        are already written,

        that they all end in 1968, with tragedy that is
also, somehow, victorious. I can't make

that story make sense. I can't square the Nashville
        of my childhood with the one that has shows

        named after it. In no way do I consider
anything resolved. The Confederate flags

in my high school parking lot are a scourge
        I did not confront. I can't tell you anything about

       leaves or trees or why anyone decides
what to do. Sometimes I still pray. But mostly

I hope that when I stoop to pick up a leaf, I will stand
       to find the forest

            gone.

MOVING DAY
a Markov Sonnet

I am born in Tennessee at the end of the '80s.
I grew up believing in the South as a concept.
I had to unlearn the first two decades of my life.

I grew up believing in the South as a concept.
I had to unlearn the first two decades of my life.
The sky seemed bluer when I moved to Oklahoma.

I had to unlearn the first two decades of my life.
The sky seemed bluer when I moved to Oklahoma.
My friends were from everywhere but Nashville.

The sky seemed bluer when I moved to Oklahoma.
My friends were from everywhere but Nashville,
and nothing made sense. My twenties flew by.

My friends were from everywhere but Nashville.
Nothing made sense. My twenties flew by
like a lark. I moved further south to Mississippi.

Nothing made sense in my twenties. I flew
like a lark, moved further south to Mississippi.
Rarely visited the coast. The sun still burns.

Like a lark I moved further south. In Mississippi
I rarely visit the coast; the burning sun
climbs the ocean each morning or evening.

I rarely visit the coast, its burning sun;
I climb the ocean each morning. In evening
the birds all disappear like old friends.

I climb the ocean each morning and evening.
All birds disappear. Like old friends,
I wait to hear a familiar voice say *hello*.

All birds will disappear like old friends.
I am waiting to hear a familiar voice say *hello*.
Won't say anything first like a child's game.

I am waiting to hear a familiar voice, say *hello*,
but won't say anything. First, like a child's game,
I'll outrun time, a friendly grasping hand,

but I won't say anything first, like a child's game.
I'll outrun time. A friendly hand, grasping,
making meaning out of all this movement.

BELIEF-MAKING

after Ada Limón, with thanks to Jon Riccio

In OK I always claimed no belief
in cardinal directions—could you tell
me if Perkins is south or west

of Stillwater? Could anyone? There's,
of course, so much people like to say:
the sun rises somewhere and goes to bed

somewhere else: as if that explains
anything. I moved south or west
of Stillwater and then I moved back

into town. I still haven't processed
all of that. It's easy, I think, to believe
the sun will keep rising, based

on prior experience, but harder
to believe that your body will
cease to exist one day: it has just

kept going for so long at this point.
In the morning, I wake up and drive
south or west (definitely: south)

and then I drive home oppositely.
One arm tans in the morning
driving south, in the afternoon

north—or maybe the other way 'round.
Try something true: treat other people
like *your* people, a compass triangulating

or re-triangulating your idea of home.
Let's re-imagine the Wild West, if we can.
No massacres. No stolen land. We'll only

try at the places that claim us, not the other
way 'round. We'll pick a direction—south,
west—we'll make it ours: we'll be made.

STATE FLAG

a Markov Sonnet

In 1894, some decisions were made by white men
having nothing and everything to do with today.
Mississippi wears its bloody history on its sleeve.

Having nothing and everything to do with today,
Mississippi wears its bloody history on its sleeve,
thumbing its nose at its citizens. We give a finger back.

Mississippi wears its bloody history on its sleeve.
Thumbing our nose at it. Citizens, we give a finger back.
Silent for years, the state finally decides to speak.

Thumbing a nose at its citizens—who give a finger back—
silent for years, the state finally decides to speak.
Out the side of its mouth, through gritted teeth.

Silent for years, the state finally decides to speak
out the side of its mouth, through gritted teeth.
The governor signs a new flag into history.

Out the side of his mouth, through gritted teeth,
the governor signs a new flag into history.
A wearied cheer goes up over the Magnolia State.

The governor signs a new flag into history.
A wearied cheer goes up over the Magnolia State;
one mayor says, *Time for waiting is over.*

A wearied cheer goes up over the Magnolia State.
One mayor says, *Time for waiting is over*;
a new shoot breaks through broken land.

One mayor says, *Time for waiting is over*;
a new shoot breaks through broken land—
a spot of green among a horizon of red.

A new shoot breaks through broken land,
a spot of green among a horizon of red.
The people keep marching forward.

A spot of green. Among a horizon of red,
the people keep marching forward,
the sun at their backs. Not quite a new day.

The people keep moving forward,
the sun at their backs. Not quite a new day.
Not while so many remain, their stories unspoken.

SELF-PORTRAIT AS MOUNTAIN OF DISCARDED LIMBS

On the tour of the antebellum mansion
where no one says the word *slave*

as if it is a curse—the guide steps
into a small room he identifies

as a guest room—tells us to follow
and that during the War this

was a surgical chamber—*That window*
he says *is where the doctors would toss*

the appendages after amputation
—and how not to imagine

that hill of limbs—the height of it—
how many soldiers were dismembered

in this place—the tour guide offers a number
I don't recall but the image

is indelible—when he asks for questions
I *mmm* and nod and stay silent—

my mouth is an arm—

ODE TO AUGUST WALKER

The week my grandmother died
I bought a 5-pack of *Mission*

Impossible movies on Blu-ray
—and a Blu-ray player. Watched

Tom Cruise grow older without seeming
to age, and all of this can be blamed

on grief, how it squirms its way into
every situation, no matter how mundane,

and you are crying outside of your apartment
door, your mother on the phone,

the one you love standing within arm's reach,
and you remember seeing the newest trailer

—how Henry Cavill cocks his fists
like he knows they could kill a man back to life.

PACKING UP THE CLASSROOM

A creek burbles behind the softball field, and
I am burying last year's grades in the backfield,
carrying papers to the dumpster where they can
degrade into pulp. The green-inked checkmarks
evaporate in midsummer winds. The principal
asks me to fill out a questionnaire. No, I have not
traveled, or gotten out of the house much; no, I
have not contracted anything; yes, I'm sure.
My room doesn't look the same: it is devoid
of students or purpose, just a container for desks
and whatever hopes remain. I yearn for kleptomania
or some excuse to lay hold of the small things
I won't remember from last year. Markers
by the SMART board, names of graduating seniors,
or what I thought I would teach them. Wave
goodbye to the principal and administrative assistant,
quietly pull out of the empty lot, imagine it
still full, buses and cars ringing the gym,
students running everywhere, unconcerned
with how close they are, no teachers
asking them to unhand each other, to stay
apart if they can. I veer onto the road, pass
fields of horses, wonder what next year
will be like: a Xerox of the last four months?
But I can't imagine what fall will yield. I lower
my windows, feel a zephyr wild my face.

I WROTE A LOVE POEM ABOUT SOMETHING YOU HATE

I have always been afraid of what my body can do:
the speed it can accrue given the right angle, the right
tools. I am skating in a backwoods rink, and all I can see
is all the things that are missing: the TMNT game cabinet

I pored over as a youth—that I poured quarters and quarters
into until my mother said that was enough—the songs I remember:
Mariah or Britney or N*SYNC now replaced with new songs, and I can
dance to either, but my brain wants one more time to hear

someone reassure me that I'll always be their baby, and when
the song changes, I want to see someone working to make
that happen, or hear them encourage everyone to grab a partner
because *this is a slow one.* Mostly, I want you to be there, too,

even if I know you would not skate. Would want you to see me
fly down the far side, even if just once, before coming to a halt
against a confetti-spackled wall, thinking that if everything changes
please, God, Someone, let this never change.

SATURDAY

On the morning my sister survives
a hurricane, I sleep so late the day
is over before I've woken up. The blinds

low in my bedroom mean it could be anytime
at all. The new bedsheets don't fit
the pillowtop, but I make do, consider

buying new sheets but don't—I'm however old
and still trying to figure out how to be a person.
I know my sister is okay because she doesn't

call, my mom doesn't text me frantically.
I am as alone as a person can be these days,
a goose who thinks they're flying by themselves

then looks around and sees a perfectly arrayed V.
Maybe we are always trailing the people we love
in our wake. Or following theirs. The meteorologists

stay quiet about Mississippi, but I know: heat,
humidity, a chance of rain every day. I walk
around the room, make coffee, say the only prayers

I can say these days: *thank you* and *thank you*
to whatever lives inside empty places,
thank you to whatever I cannot name

that keeps sending their presence outward,
the point the geese follow because they know
it's where they're headed next.

EPITHALAMIUM FOR MO AND SUSANNA

Some pray for rain and wait, expecting
a return for their actions. Some act.

Some claim that love will save them
and some that there is no love. Each of

these choices are certainly chooseable but
I tell you this: those who believe

and do nothing are lesser than those who
act with no belief. Those who pour love

into the lives of those around them
are surely greater than those who hoard

their love. For any two who believe
there is something worth salvaging

in this misbegotten world—that *must*
be love. Poets, it is said, only write

of death and love, for what else
is there to write about? I tell you this:

poets only write about one thing:
love and how it moves within them.

The world we see may not last, but
love must. Many wish to live forever

but the closest the world has come
is when a poet writes about the one

they love. I love you both, my sisters,
and with whatever power poetry may

possess, I bless your union. May your
joys be more joyous because of each other;

may your griefs be less grievous. When
your anger is stoked by an unkind word

or a thoughtless action, do not think
of this day—for this day will surely fade—

but recall a brighter memory—a sunlit
walk, a morning conversation, how you

feel when the other comes home from work,
takes off her shoes, and you ask: "How was

your day?" The smallest moments will add up,
one flower and one flower and one flower.

What is a marriage if not the act of choosing
the other each day? A choice like that

cannot be unmade. That choice *must* be love.

TRAVELOGUE

I tell stories that are sun-dappled and bright

and you see the light, the visits to far-off

lands, the language I never learned, exotic

tales. I hold back all the darkness. The day

Jon and I got lost for hours. The countless

nights we didn't cry only because the other

was in the room. The night that all of us did

cry, really let go, because how could we not?

I don't mention these when reminiscing

with my parents. It feels gauche to mention

them now. What am I trying to say? I like

to imagine, in my retellings, that you are there

with me, my shadow, that like I learned in Sunday school,

like God's grace, somehow, you were with me *preveniently*,

that there was a hole in my life that you were meant

to fill. When Jon and I finally made it to Alexander

Nevksy Cathedral, we sighed. We hugged. The day

was saved. We found the one subway entrance

we knew by heart in this city, and waited quietly

like the older passengers, as it carried us home.

FIRST, SECOND, THIRD PERSON

with a line from Robert Creeley
in memory of D.R.

I am still stuck on poetry, I said, once,
a lifetime ago, or not too long ago,

depending on who *you* are, or who *I*
is, when *you* reads this or *I* writes it.

And it's true even now. An old friend
writes that she has moved beyond stanzas,

and all I can think is—how? I am trying,
even now, to decipher the mysteries

of a couplet, of *an amulet and quick surprise*
part of me wants to say, borrowing

another poet's words, or stealing
like great artists are often said to do,

but I'm not sure that's true. The words
stay the same whether they are mine

or someone else's. *Nothing is new
under the sun, cries the Preacher* was

always one of my favorite verses, even
as a child, even young in faith and life,

believing so much in something I cannot
comprehend, like stanzas, like God,

like this life I have found myself happily
wandering into. I hope you found it too.

BIRDS, WORLD

On some days, it feels like
I have nothing to add
to the conversation that is

this world. On most days,
I am a seed being dropped
on clay, a dry and parched

place, where the birds,
such as they are—grackle,
corvid, humming—pick

my body up and move it
somewhere else, or devour
me whole. On a few choice

days, I have clarity, I'm sure
I do. Or at least, I believe
that I did at one time. Or maybe

I have always been unsure
of what I am doing. And
will always be this way.

And if there is not comfort
in that thought, exactly, there is
something like surety there,

which, considering the world,
such as it is—devastation mounting
on devastation—I'll take.

I'll take it all and keep it to myself.

MORNING RITUALS

based on a line by Jessica Guzman

The Clay Aikens feared dying first, the thirst
that lack of spotlight yields. He started as a single
Clay Aiken, the one we all knew with the smiling face
and aw-shucks demeanor, but each day he woke
after coming in second on *AI*, a new Clay Aiken appeared
beside the last one until he had to rent an entire block
of apartments for all the Clay Aikens he was. He sent one
Clay Aiken to Broadway, one to *Dancing with the Stars*, another
ran for Congress—unsuccessfully. The Clay Aikens became a father,
grew their hair out, lived their life in peace. All this wanting
became a bore. The Clay Aikens settled down, let their dog out
each morning, smiled when Raleigh fetched the paper.
The Clay Aikens never see their face under headlines,
and this excites them. Somewhere, Ruben Studdard is alone,
crying. This, too, excites them. The neighbors
barely recognize them as The Clay Aikens anymore,
That's just Clay, they say, and it's true. The Clay Aikens
go to yoga at 6:15 every morning, punctual as Ryan Seacrest,
though perhaps not as well-groomed these days. In their lululemons,
the Clay Aikens appear average; their classmates point and say,
Clay Aikens, they're just like us behind their hands
and into their cellphones. The Clay Aikens go home,
search "Clay Aiken" on Twitter, check their Google Alerts.
The number of tweets about Clay Aiken is less than
the number of Clay Aikens, and Google is tired
of keeping up with the Clay Aikens. The first
Clay Aiken pulls out an old Philips VCR, watches the dust
dance as he blows on the small of its back and plugs
it into his flatscreen. From behind a portrait of himself,

he pulls a tape labeled "LORD OF RINGS RETURN OF KING"
and pushes it into the VCR's mouth. The VCR gulps.
Clay hits the triangle, watches himself
sing Billy Joel, Elton John, The Beatles, Simon
and Garfunkel. In the stale air of his apartment,
Clay Aiken feels alive for a moment. The other Clay Aikens
fall silent. No pleas, no songs. When the tape regurgitates,
Clay forcefeeds the VCR again. He wakes
the next morning, still by himself, makes coffee for one,
and a muffin. Kisses his child on one of the soft spaces
where, someday soon, bones will grow. "Not yet," he says.
"Not today." At the door, the mailman hands Clay
Aiken an envelope that reads *I blame you. xoxo R.S.*
Next morning, there is a Clay Aiken in bed
with Clay Aiken and nothing to watch on TV.

RUNNING WITH THE BULL

The convicted murderer is comatose,
but that's last season, backstory,

Previously On—there is family
to consider, his and mine, what it says

about me that I spend hours inside
his world, how these windows

his sister is waiting behind look
like the prison bars he knew for years;

the dream sequences feel like my dreams
or memories I had removed years ago:

it all comes back to some screen
and the ways I can live inside it;

after 45 minutes the convicted murderer
wakes, batting his eyelashes like

a French skunk or a mouse in a polka-dot
dress, a rabbit, a desperate man. I think

like this too much: metaphors no one
understands are gibberish. When

the credits roll I stay seated because
personhood is enticing but trees have

the right idea: face me toward
a window, let me practice losing

my leaves every autumn. Let me
never grow anew each spring

the green I believe must recur.

A HISTORY OF GARDENING

Both of my grandfathers have gardens
—roses, zucchini, okra—beauty
and utility. I would like a garden to call
out to once a week, after dark,
how are you? If the flowers crook
their stems, if the bushes stop
rustling, I will take that as answer.
Keep watch over them as a trellis.

I will take my time, bend into
their ears, whisper sweet somethings,
tuck them in, pat their beds with water
from a metal can. Even after death,
my grandfathers' work continues.
The gardens return what they have received.

Some people can do a lot with a small
plot, but I am useless even in an expanse.
The ground is patient, it will do what it can,
but first: action is required. Rain may fall,
may wash the ground or flood us all away.
I could wither, could decide not to stay.
My grandfathers have gardens; I will have what remains.

A HISTORY OF GARDENING

My grandfathers have gardens; I have what remains
—another winter in an uncold place, my parents
waiting the other side of a phone, an empty table
in an empty room. I say make what you will
of imagery. Somewhere else, a hawk pierces
the corona of the sun. A car bisects perfectly
a suburban driveway. There are hands, hand-offs,
and hand-me-downs. They all work singlehandedly.

I can tell you a story about gardens, a history
of peering over a grandfather's shoulder; I can
make you believe I know what I am saying.
But when my sweat falls to the earth, it is rejected
out-of-hand, and I don't mind. I straighten my back,
crack my neck, and go inside for the day.

When I write this down, I mean to say something small
and adjacent to the truth. The way a watering can
is meant to service a patch of land, not an expanse.
Summer means to warm and stop, not pass into fall
and winter. We want our garden friends to settle down,
pick our yard for their home. When they move away
we let them. Make do with their new-green remains.

LANDSCAPE WITH A CALM
after Nicolas Poussin

How nice, to imagine a calm
day—to see oneself shepherding
through a greenspace by any lake
or pond, your neighbor's house
reflecting in the waters, so calm
that it belies what turmoil
waits when you get home, what
your parents will think of your life
's work, how hungry you will feel,
and how you spent all day with calm
animals who never knew what
they were destined for: to feed
a farmer's belly or be shorn
to share their warmth with another,
and really who wouldn't see a calm
and think to paint it, especially
when it is so hard to come by;
how strange it is to think
of this concept, how unlikely
anything approaching the word calm
has seemed for years now, when
the world seems so eager to run
toward everything but—and how
strange it is to see a word so familiar
be used so unfamiliarly: *a* calm,
as if the word were not description
but an entire world of its own, a place
you could visit, given enough time
(which we do not have) or money

(which we also do not have), calm
like the sheep I am never tending,
the house I will never see, the lake
that reminds me most of a subdivision
for wealthy inhabitants, their prim
and proper lawns, their greenways, how calm
it must seem for them on a normal day,
and how much they must fear losing
—how quickly all of this can leave us
like a shepherd leaving 99 to find 1 sheep,
how that story was meant to calm
us, how it makes me itch now, and yet
who doesn't want to run away and still
be found—who doesn't want their shepherd
searching only for them? and why not
have this day be one of—what else!—calm?

CALL AN EXALTATION

We raced the storm
back home. Fled

the town we might
call a second home

this fall, depending
on our government,

regulations, what
officials *think* might

be best. But by
all accounts, all

we can do is wait
now. A bird nests

on my parents' porch,
just below the gutter,

and my father takes
photos because he

dares not bring them
inside. He has become

a watcher of birds,
and I envy his ability

to find something new
to interest him every

few years. I am still
stuck on poetry. Did

you know whenever
a poem is written,

a tornado—God's
finger—is beheaded,

some angel salved,
a hood ornament

buffed, shining like
the feathers of a baby

bird, fresh out of their
egg, a flock, perhaps

of larks, which some
call an exaltation?

FIREFALL

History says that a man stood at the bottom of a cascade and, as a signal, intoned: *Let the fire fall*. As if this could be done by mere hands; exposure to the elements teaches even the noblest skeptic that fire burns through everything given enough time. Anything can become historical; all it must do is stop. History says—and History is always saying something—an entrepreneur built a hotel on top of a mountain that History, decades later, would call a park. There were bonfires, and when those died down, the tradition of boys kicking flames over a cliff became a sensation that people would pay to experience. History says the park caught up with the spectacle, disallowed it, called it a fraud, unnatural. The rangers must not have seen it with their eyes, must have heard rather than known the splendor of it. When the last fire fell, it was snowy, and no one was there as witness. No one to tell the fire what to do, no lenses to capture, even momentarily, the weight of what can be, still falling.

A HISTORY OF GENEALOGIES

My father's grandfather was born Rutherford B. Hayes Osborne, after a president that most don't recall in any way. First president to win despite losing the popular election, showing the American story of democracy to be just that. He ended Reconstruction, too, and I suppose it is the latter that makes him a proper name for a child born in the South at the beginning of the twentieth century. But my great-grandfather thought his birth certificate read Bea Hazel because some nurse mistook him for a baby girl, misread or misheard what the doctor said. So he went by B. H. his whole life. Maybe he blushed when asked what the letters stood for. Maybe like Truman's S, he said they stood for nothing. Still, it is almost magical in its story-ness, first told to me years ago by my father while I sat on the big freezer, legs dangling, his face stuck in a PC's guts, as he pulled out arteries and reattached organs, rebooted the heart with a few clicks. *What are the chances of that? What luck!* My father stared me down, and simply said, *There's no such thing as luck, only faith.* And I agreed with him then. But I would say now, I would have my younger self say—there are stories, pieces of luck and faith strung together until you can't tell the difference.

PROMISE DART

after Damien Hirst

for my grandmothers and my mother, too

[TEMPLE]

My sister swims with stingrays, while I wade through waves,
waiting to see what will happen. My grandfather,
with his transition lenses and hair white as an X-ray, lets them
kiss his back, their mouths suctioning his skin.

[DEATH EXPLAINED]

Genesis says that God cut a calf and sheep and dove in two
and walked between them. *If I don't keep my word, may this be
done to me.* And what could Abraham say to that?
When he awoke the next day, he felt the same, but knew
that he was different. The desert landscape beckoned.

[A THOUSAND YEARS]

When my grandfather spoke to me, I laughed, all nerves
and teenage circumspection. I could not imagine his life,
or see it as in a movie: the marriage, the kids, the years spent
at the same job. I kept adding them up and losing the number.

[IN AND OUT OF LOVE]

Alzheimer's is irretrievable once spoken. It hovers
in the air between you and the speaker. Flutters
in your ear canal: a fly nattering at your eardrum,
a bat smashing itself into a closed window.

[THE KINGDOM OF THE FATHER]
Winter cold outside the screen door, and my mother and grandmother
waiting. A clock on the wall the only thing that changes. No snow
to dampen the doorways, just the wind and the night air calling,
a phone no one wants to answer, that keeps ringing.

[HYMN]
The heart, the lungs, the intestines all intact: the eyes that see,
the pumping guts. Only the brain truly exposed to the elements—
shown to be as fragile as it looks, sulci and gyri willing
to stretch into nothingness given the right leisure.
A taffy-pulling machine would be more forgiving.

[THE TRANQUILITY OF SOLITUDE (FOR GEORGE DYER)]
When learning to swim, it is important to exhale.
At all times practice the in, the out. Tell yourself
you are in control, even in the ocean. If you stay
calm, you can backstroke through breakers, breathing.

[THE PHYSICAL IMPOSSIBILITY OF DEATH
          IN THE MIND OF SOMEONE LIVING]
God told Moses what to do, and he did it. Walking across
dry seabank, the wonders of it, we have recreated in our
everyday aquariums, our wild galleries. A parade of fish
arrayed before the children's eyes. So close they can see
their own arms reflected in the shark's dark pupils.

[THE SACRED HEART OF JESUS]

The pain was not that he was gone, but that he had been dead
for years, and we were left to carry his body like a casket
with no grave to be lowered into. It is enough to know our shoulders
sighed when he went. Our backs gave up their stupor. We fell to
knees grown weak from overuse, the bending and the raising up.

[MOTHER AND CHILD (DIVIDED)]

I felt cut off from the loss my mother owned the way I possess
arms, legs, the etcetera of body. I kept siphoning emotions
into my face, the twist of a frown, the mechanics of waterworks,
the slow realization that someday I will know what she knows.

[SAINT SEBASTIAN, EXQUISITE PAIN]

When I hear *pool*, I remember a stranger's backyard, learning
and failing to learn the perfect butterfly kick, the trick of when
to come up for air and when to keep going. Not my grandfather,
bearded, already losing himself in the sun beside blue waters.

[VERITY]

Samuel's mother prayed silently for years until he was born. Saul
scoffed, and then his Jonathan was lost. Solomon the Wise nearly
cut a child in two. And above them I hear David bleating, pleading,
his son caught like a ram in a thicket, his shadow dancing
among the leaves and branches. *Absalom! O my Absalom!*

[SOME COMFORT GAINED FROM THE ACCEPTANCE
OF THE INHERENT LIES IN EVERYTHING]

I thought grief would split me and move on, but nothing moved
in to the place where my grandfather had resided. When I think
of him, I see a picture that my mother took: he's in a suit,
holding his wife, and I can hardly tell he doesn't know where he is.

[THE TRUE ARTIST HELPS THE WORLD
BY REVEALING MYSTIC TRUTHS]

My grandmother picked up her Bible, found something in the words
that reminded her, perhaps, of a day when she saw a stranger across
a room and crossed it, or waited for him to cross. When they touched
they were encased in glass, preserved for generations.

[TWO SIMILAR SWIMMING FORMS
IN ENDLESS MOTION (BROKEN)]

The mind goes back to the last moment when the eyes were his,
before the circle of his mind became a curved line, before
the trap door in his head opened, plunged him into another room
with no windows or doors, a word problem with no good answers.

[FOR THE LOVE OF GOD]

I placed a rose on my grandfather's casket before the caretaker
began his work. The country cemetery—a green yard with equidistant
stones lodged into the earth—billowed out to the road and the church.
In the car's rearview mirror, they looked like teeth in a skull.

[BECAUSE I CAN'T HAVE YOU I WANT YOU]
Jesus said, *Cast your nets* and they were cast. He said, *Other side*
and they were recast. And there were fish. When Peter looked up
to thank Jesus, He was already ashore, cooking breakfast. So much
to do, so Peter got to work. When he looked up again, Jesus was gone,
the brazier still smoking. A note written in sand half washed away.

[UP, UP AND AWAY]
I heard a story about my grandfather: he was in a battlefield
laden with landmines; he mis-stepped and shrapnel found purchase
in his back. Doctors were too frightened to remove it, so it became
part of him. Later, my mother said this story was wrong: it was
a child's go-kart accident. Or it was neither of these truths.

[THE PURSUIT OF OBLIVION]
Driving back: blur of roadside trees, houses and businesses, subdivisions
and then we are home. Like a pet bird, we squawk when the cage is
covered, throwing the world into darkness. Other side
of the cloth, everything is there, but we can't imagine—the same
furniture in the living room. All our books still painted with dust.

[THE KISS OF DEATH]
This is what I write about: my mother; a bull's heart
cleaved by sterling silver; the feeling the heart senses
when it is not split, but left hovering in the chest as a lacuna.
My mother stares at me, and we both look like we're smiling.

INSIDE JOKES

I *have* been to Cades Cove
despite what you might have heard

me tell my mother, endlessly,
as she recounts another trip

the family is taking without me,
without *us*, now, and I tell her

the truth—It's fine—because
she deserves to see the Badlands

and Maine, even Halifax, and
who am I to tell her not to

just because I also want to be free
of the things that hold me down:

a lease agreement, a contract
for the school year, inertia if I had to guess—

look, I didn't see a bear at Cades Cove,
and I've never been one for the outdoors;

even when a Boy Scout, I mostly avoided
campouts, couldn't last a year,

but I want to write about more than
sadness and history, if I can—I want

the joy, too, the laughs, the moments
when I look at you and say, *hey,*

and nothing else can stretch forever
if we let them; I am driving home

and even though I-40 is not
on the itinerary, and everyone

knows it, I tell my parents I am
driving through Pegram because

I like the way it sounds on my tongue,
and I like hearing my mother laugh

and say, *You're a little off course,*
aren't you? I am, but I'm coming home.

GHOST BALLET

My hometown has suspicious
taste in communal art: there is

a rollercoaster by the river
—the one that flooded

its banks in 2010, which
no one remembers unless

you were there; unless
you felt water pouring

two days straight and worried
what would be left—and

I guess what I mean is
there are 2 tracks of red

steel tangled not like lovers
but like the arms of a robot,

or the kinds of minds
that see a body on their steps

as a threat, legislate
rights only to those

who look like them
and none else. It's called

Ghost Ballet because that's
the only kind of ballet

left in Nashville. It's
called *Ghost Ballet* because

the afterlife funds the arts
more than Nashville.

It's called *Ghost Ballet*
because I and you and we

can never return to where
we once were—always

ghosting our way through
the city, down Hermitage Ave.

toward Broad, and there it waits
on the far bank: a solo dancer

with the lights turned off,
a ballerina in an empty room.

A HISTORY OF PIANO SHOWROOMS

One day a piano appeared in our den,
not like the grands in the showroom
where my sister took lessons, practiced

scales with each hand, building strength
in her fingers; Mom sat

in the soundproof room with her while
I wandered the floor, using one finger to pick
my way up and down the keys, or sliding my hand

across like how I imagined real piano-players did
for emphasis, or to end a rousing piece.

Mo played "Fur Elise," learned
"Somewhere Out There" from *An American
Tale*, gave up after a few years.

She had her books and "Chopsticks"—
she'd be fine. Now, when everyone's back

home, I find myself at that same piano,
plinking out a carol or a new pop song
for us to sing along to. The showroom isn't there

anymore, but a guy on PBS can teach you
to play piano, for only five payments of $19.99.

Watch YouTube videos. Look up how
to play an F chord. Put your thumb
on the first note, then count to three

on the white keys, then five. Or maybe
the showroom is still there, waiting.

WISE

Picture the perfect day: nothing troubles you
and no one asks you for anything. The world is

a terrible place, and beautiful, and I am so afraid
of most everything. I want certainty. I want

uncertainty that is manageable, that I can bite
into pieces small enough to swallow whole

with my nightly pills. I want to brush my teeth
each day—at least twice—and let that be enough

for the world to continue unbothered. I cannot name
the bird that alit outside my friend's window while

I was feeding her cat and she was stuck at a far-off
place, nursing a bad back, re-learning to walk, a thing

we all learned without even remembering, but which
is so difficult to master a second time. A marvel,

this body we are given. A mystery, this body, and
what it contains—our heart, both literal and metaphysical;

our mind; every feeling we receive from nerve endings
and synapses. On my perfect day I am embodied

by a fox, my namesake. I run through a forest
that is also a library. I read every leaf on each tree.

They tell me their stories so slowly I forget them
by the time I finish reading. But I remember

what matters most: the feeling of bark on my warm
snout, how the wind whips my whiskers, my paws

on bare ground and nothing standing between
the world I know and the world that exists.

THE IDEA OF CUTTING A *V* INTO YOUR TOENAIL
IS AN OLD WIVES' TALE

My father told me a lie
and I believed him: in ancient

Greek *apokalupsis* means
an uncovering, or *a revelation*,

an apocalypse I keep
returning to because it is important

for me to tell you,
to bring apocalypse

to you—it is the watermark
of everything written

these days, when the sky
is orange the way

a campfire is, or the way
a used fireplace might be,

or the way a fire makes it,
and if apocalypse is not

an end but a peeling back
of dead skin, a debriding

of a wound, then why look
at any apocalypse as necessarily

tragic instead of seeing
what could be: once

all was one, landmasses
huddled together,

and we have been
working toward that again:

the waters rise un
-ceasingly, there is one

ocean again. Our bodies float
to make the new Pangaea, and

finally we will all be one.

EPITHALAMIUM FOR PANDEMIC WEDDING

All spring we make plans only for them to change
before summer: we have a venue, then a smaller
one, and then: there will be people, but all our
friends will watch from home. We arrange
everything with our families, ask them to stay
inside for a few weeks: My parents have birds
to keep them occupied, and there's TV: words
said in a certain order to help us feel okay

or remind us everything isn't. I keep wanting
to talk about love. The past arrives to push
closed each door that reads *sound, image,
rhyme*. We see the room once, light slanting
through the windows, then the room, hushed
and barely occupied, and our marriage

begins. We smile for pictures taken by your
sister, my father. My sister plays pastor
one more time—there are three people here who are
not technically family, though they are close
enough to be. It is a day of joy in the middle
of a sea of sadness that has gotten so deep we cannot
touch its bottom, its current quick and rage-inducing.
I keep wanting to talk about your beautiful
face, or let you know that this poem is, yes,
somehow a love poem. I can write a poem
about anything except my own happiness,
it seems, but I am trying to write into that
as much as I can. We got married in the

afternoon, and then got drinks at a gas station
you frequented as a kid. We got snacks
from Walmart. Hibachi to go. That night
we couldn't sleep; I recited each president
from memory. It didn't help us sleep
any better, but it didn't hurt. I don't like
to romanticize the past (or I only romanticize
the past)

       but that was, in spite of everything else
happening in the world, a singular, unblemished day.

I SLEEP LIKE A VAMPIRE ON HIS SIDE

you tell me, my arms crossed
over my chest the same way

my father would sleep on Sunday
afternoons, newspaper crumpled

against his ribs, turned to
the Sports section, the sound

of engines revving as high
as they can while men slingshot

around a gray oval—am I
being too sentimental

about the past again? *It's called
a track, son*, I almost hear

him say, though I'm not sure
he ever did. It's amazing

to me how much we have learned
about ourselves together,

you and me—my crossed arms,
obviously, your bedhead,

the things I thought so normal
that they need not be spoken

now shown to be an oddity,
specific to my childhood,

how quickly a new normal
can make itself known. I talk

in my sleep, and you snore
sometimes, and we both

hate waking up early, but
we'll do it. We have to.

The sun we watch rise
may be orange or purple;

its reflection in your eyes
is still a miracle. I count

backwards to help myself
fall asleep, or I sing a song

so my brain can't sing its own,
and when I wake, I wake

slowly, until my brain remembers
it is here with you and

the day takes on the shape
of the comics my father

would clip out of each Sunday
paper, the rest of the news

stacked in a pile underneath
an end table. The dedication

was so remarkable to me,
and still is, even if the stacks

are gone. They are gone
and they are never coming back.

TEACHER OF A YEAR

The newsman we like is talking again
about how—relatively—safe this year

has been for teachers, but all I hear
is the relief in your voice, rising,

as you tell me the test is negative.
I say a prayer of thanks, positive

for once that this something
I thank is responsible. Gratitude

feels impossible this year. Should
I have suggested teaching

to you, too? Hindsight is
a poor instructor. Each day we survive

feels like a miracle. Like
parting seas while turning

them into wine. The fish
all drunk, glazed and glass-eyed

at the bottom of bottles,
looking like my students

most days, or what I can make
of their faces above school-issue

masks that feel like a T-shirt
cut up for a school project.

I try to keep my mouth shut
so I can keep my job, but

occasionally I let them know
how dire things are, that

just because they aren't
experiencing a pain does not

mean it is not happening.
I yell about it, and they call me

hysterical, probably, or crazy.
They think I am exaggerating,

and I wish I were. No one wants
to believe bad news. It takes

too long to process until
eventually it becomes the past.

One day, this year will be
the past. I think I will miss

most spending so much time
with you.

124 DAYS AFTER THE APOCALYPSE

I go back to work. I tire
more easily. I am trying to be
strong, for you, for everyone.

I go back to work, tired.
The students notice. Suggest coffee:
strong, for me, for everyone.
It's a nice idea, but what about

the students? Notice: coffee suggests
a problem: world-weariness
is a nice idea but what about
self-weariness? Am I

the problem? World-weariness
is common these days. And so I try
self-weariness. I am
not certain of anything, but that's

common these days. If you try
to convince the world you're fine,
it won't be certain of anything. That's
just truth. A bird flying overhead

cannot convince me the world is fine,
but it can get close. I still love the moon,
it's true: that bird flying overhead
can hold onto its secrets: flight;

how to get close to the moon;
or look at the sun without crying.
These are the secrets I hold: flying
doesn't scare me but it makes me sick.

I look at the sun and start to cry:
I can't be strong for everyone.
That scares me sick; I want to be
finished; start beginning the world; undazed.

WHEN THE DAILY NUMBER OF NEW INFECTIONS CLIMBS INTO THE SIX FIGURES FOR THE FIRST TIME, I WRITE IT ON MY WHITEBOARD EACH MORNING

and when my students ask me what it is, I tell them,
and I can see in their faces they are not sure
they want to believe me. I don't blame them.
I don't want to believe me either. Can anything be

rebuilt after so much destruction? Whenever I hear
of some family's house burning to the ground,
the story always ends when the community
rallies around them, provides new clothes, a warm

place to stay for a night or two, but surely
there must come a day when that family is
forgotten, when another house burns down,
when a tornado rips through a neighboring

subdivision, when even the people of God
must move on, not out of callousness but because
we were only built to hold so much suffering.
And what to do when the suffering is so great,

so manifold that we cannot comprehend it?
The students eventually stop arguing with me
about the severity of a given disease, whether
or not to wear the school-mandated masks—

stop mentioning their weekend plans, because they know
I am not going to tell them everything will be okay.
In the middle of crossing a river, it is difficult
to think of the other side as anything other than mirage.

In the middle of a long tunnel, or the depths
of a cavern, light becomes a memory quickly fading,
an idea more than a reality, until you break through
to the other side. I tell my students, *We're not there yet.*

ANT BED

I don't know—I didn't know—what it was,
　　　　this patch of dirt across the crease between

the wall where my only functioning window sits
　　　　and the floor, near where a student sits in every

class, a surefire way to get noticed
　　　　in a high school classroom: to exist and also

to be out of place, like I felt in middle school
　　　　and high school, too—until I didn't, until it felt

like I could just exist without any kind of notice,
　　　　and yet when a student said, so surprised, *you don't know*

what an ant bed is?, how to explain I am not,
　　　　will never be, who they think I might be,

am still an indoor kid trying to win whatever
　　　　affection might be thrown my way, however

small or ineffective it might be, however
　　　　slight. No, I don't. But I can make

an uneducated guess: imagine row
　　　　after row of workers after a long day of—

teaching? I'd joke but no—gathering, right?
　　　　for their queen? Ants have those, I've heard,

or maybe misremembered from some
        movie. *Like an ant hill*, my students say now,

gathering to look at it, though we shouldn't (gather),
        and yet, what to make of it when outside comes in?

Not quite uncanny but still unusual to see a little hive-
        in-the-making, a functioning society, so unlike—how else

to say this?—my classroom, this county, state, nation.
        It is best to stay in the image, my teachers might have said,

to focus on the ant bed, the texture of it, how it moved
        within itself, tiny workers so happy to do what they are

told. And if they die in this service it is considered
        not at all. The work continues. A single ant can carry the world

if it must, but it needs a colony to make a bed their home.

A LOVE POEM

When we started dating, I told my wife
cats cannot feel love, *that*—and I quote—
any emotion you see in their eyes
is simply a reflection of your own
peering back at you.

                       Now I find myself
tucked over a food bowl, spooning
moist pats of salmon onto my fingers
and presenting it to our cat as if he were
a god and I a humble supplicant
with the merest offering. I don't know
if he loves me (though I think he might),
but I know I love him, and as I am
so often wrong about things, my wife
likes to mention this to me.

                         Did you
ever think you would love two cats?
she asks. And I answer, of course, *No.*
What else could I say? I am trying
to fall in love with the world. I am
trying my best. I am tired all the time
but when a cat curls onto my stomach
or across my lap, I feel loved. Of course
I do. To feel otherwise would be preposterous.
I feel my cat's sandpaper tongue
and it feels like a benison, matins
and vesper in one, and I like the holiest
child of some not-entirely-holy deity.
I am praying he may be eternal. I am

sending him all my love and receiving
something like love in return, a warmth
and a breadth more real than most people
have shown.

        He will recover, I'm sure,
and we will have many years of this to go.
I will continue in awe of him, in love
with a being whose own capacities are
simply unknowable: a bottomless pond;
the heights of the sky; the sea.

"THE NUNS HAVE BEEN CALLED!"

The skin of my hands is cracking,
the sky is gray as dust, and our cat

is sick. I want the world to continue
but not like this. A new year always

makes me mad because it promises
something different but rarely

gives it: a rising rate of unemployment,
or inflation, or infection, and it's been

years of this and yet—when our friend
tells us the nuns have been called:

how not to smile at that? The image
both beatific and beautiful,

this group of women we've never met
calling forth for healing. How not to

believe in the ability of some community
to make something *ex nihilo*, out of all

this nothing to bring forth new life
that, unlike the new year, will never

leave me feeling dust-gray, ashen
like this perfect sky, black and white

as the habits we'll never put on,
the feelings we'll pour into our lives

like water, like lotion, bringing something
like moisture to this dry and desert land.

ENOUGH

On the day the government opened its doors
so you could make my name yours, we booked

a honeymoon—two years late but worth it
for the way your voice bounced and filled

with light as you discussed the plans we were,
finally, making—our future a certainty

like the return of severe thunderstorms next
Tuesday or maybe Wednesday—like Miami's

coastline will be deleted—like how we will
continue to love each other even as all of this

continues to be true—the world is ending
and we have found each other and made that enough.

WORLD-ENDING

a golden shovel after Tracy K. Smith's "Credulity"

It rained all day. Nothing went right. We
argued with each other—do we believe
each other when we speak? we agree; we
do—and then made up. I like the light in your eyes when you are
explaining yourself, how the act of giving
context is also an act of love, how we ourselves
continue the good work, this love we made from nothing. Away,
away, the fussing and fighting. Do not darken our door today. And
it rained? So? What can the rain do? That old so-and-so
had better move on. And of course, all of this makes me think of it
: the world, its end. Not a future-thing, something that merely feels
far-off: the current ending of our world: the good
and all the rest. It may end poorly, as such things often do. Or. Our
world may continue on. There may be an after, after all, like bodies
turning into earth, my bones swimming
with yours and making soil that will let us intermingle together
for something like eternity. Imagine that. In
Sunday school, they always told us the end could come suddenly: any afternoon
could do it—they couldn't prepare me, us, for all this light,
this heat, the way the world would heave its own sigh as if the
end could not come quickly enough, like an annoying piece of music
stuck in my head. I hum it all day until you tell me *stop*. I stop. That
is also a form of love. I am waiting for what comes next, what enters
in the door—like a cowboy in an old saloon, like our
cat scurrying the corner to get to the food bowl quicker—or peeks in a window
to make itself known. The end has come, but I am not as
sad as I expected. I listen to sad music, I plan to take a walk far
away, for the exercise. I plan to exercise. From
what I've been told, it is necessary to prevent the

end of all things. Do I quibble with T.S. Eliot? Very well, I quibble. What if mermaid voices
are the only ones left? What if the world ends with silence? What to make of that
level of anti-climax? While we were busy watching sausage get made
the rest of the factory burned around our ears. We walk outside of it
and sit on the grass. The flames describe a story into the clouds. As
if the arsonist were an artist after all, and our
world his palette. We keep trying to find a place that is all our own
but no such place exists. Not even in our minds
are we alone. Not really. We hold each other close, for we are
all we have. We keep each other safe from
the world that hunts our love with none and with every reason.

NOTES

"Moving Day" and "State Flag" are both Markov sonnets, a form first developed by George Abraham.

"Belief-Making" is based on a writing prompt from Jon Riccio and uses Ada Limon's "Time Is On Fire" as a jumping-off point.

"Running with the Bull" was inspired by *Rectify*, a TV show about a man who is released from death row after seventeen years.

"Promise Dart" is a pecha kucha, a form developed by Terrance Hayes and taking as its inspiration the pecha kucha presentation. The poem consists of twenty "slides," each based on a work by the same artist, in this case the English artist Damien Hirst.

ACKNOWLEDGMENTS

Books do not happen in a vacuum or with a single person. I am forever indebted to Casie Dodd for taking a chance on my poetry. This book would not exist without her thoughtful work in putting it out into the world. Thank you!

I am grateful to all of the editors who gave the following poems their first publication:

Big Muddy: "A History of Gardening" ("Both of my grandfathers have gardens"), originally published as "On Gardening"
CutBank Literary Magazine: "Self-Portrait as Mountain of Discarded Limbs"
decomP magazinE: "A History of Decks"
EcoTheo Review: "Call an Exaltation"
Gravel: "After sunlight," originally published as "After—"
Hobart: "Morning Rituals"
Jet Fuel Review: "Snow"
Mayday Magazine: "Re:"
Mid/South Anthology: "Belief-Making" and "Epithalamium for Pandemic Wedding"
The Missouri Review: "Running with the Bull" was published as part of their "Poem of the Week" feature
Nat. Brut.: "A History of Trees"
Redactions: Poetry & Poetics: "A History of Gardening" ("My grandfathers have gardens; I have what remains")
Scrawl Place: "Ghost Ballet"
The Shore: "Saturday" and "Ode to August Walker"
Tar River Poetry: "Drone"
Tinderbox Poetry Journal: "Firefall"

To my family—Mom, Dad, Grandma—your support has meant so much to me over the years. I could not have made it here without you. Mo and Susanna, thank you for phone calls while you're driving and for letting me officiate your wedding. To my extended family, especially my two writing Aunts, Beth and Nikki—thank you for showing me that writing is something I can do with my life. Uncle Mike, Uncle Brian, Brenna, and Daniel: I wish I was around more for weekly dinners and game nights. I love you.

To all of the teachers in my life, especially Dr. Rummage and Dr. Philip, thank you for all you taught me. To Lisa Lewis, Rebecca Hazelton, and Rose McLarney, thank you for helping me grow into the writer I am today. To all of the professors at the Center for Writers, but especially to Angela Ball, Rebecca Morgan Frank, and Adam Clay: thank you so much.

To my cohorts at OSU: Mike, Andy, Emma, Dillon, Nate, Monique, and many, many others—thank you! At the Center for Writers, I could not have made it through without the help of many wonderful friends, most especially Jessica Guzman, Hannah Dow, Matthew Schmidt, Jon Riccio, and Mary Spooner.

To those I adventured with in lands both real and fantastical—Kyle, Jenni, Jen, Addison, Fletcher, Hayden, Ford, Joe, JB, and Arthur—thank you for your friendship and camaraderie! Many thanks to Ben and Emily for being good neighbors and better friends.

To Mary: so much of this book would not be the same without you. Thank you for loving me and allowing me to love you in return. You are and will always be the shade of my heart. Thank you for convincing me that I could love *four* cats: Patrina, Gwen, Pizza Roll—I love you. Edward, I love and miss you.

TODD OSBORNE is a poet and teacher originally from Nashville. He is a feedback editor for *Tinderbox Poetry Journal* and a poetry reader for *Memorious*. His poems have been featured at *Scrawl Place*, *CutBank*, *The Missouri Review*, *Tar River Poetry*, and *EcoTheo Review*. He lives in Hattiesburg, Mississippi, with his wife and their three cats.